# Amazing Lions In The Wild
# Beautiful Predators

Mick.E.Purcell

ISBN-13: 978-1722137854
ISBN-10: 1722137851

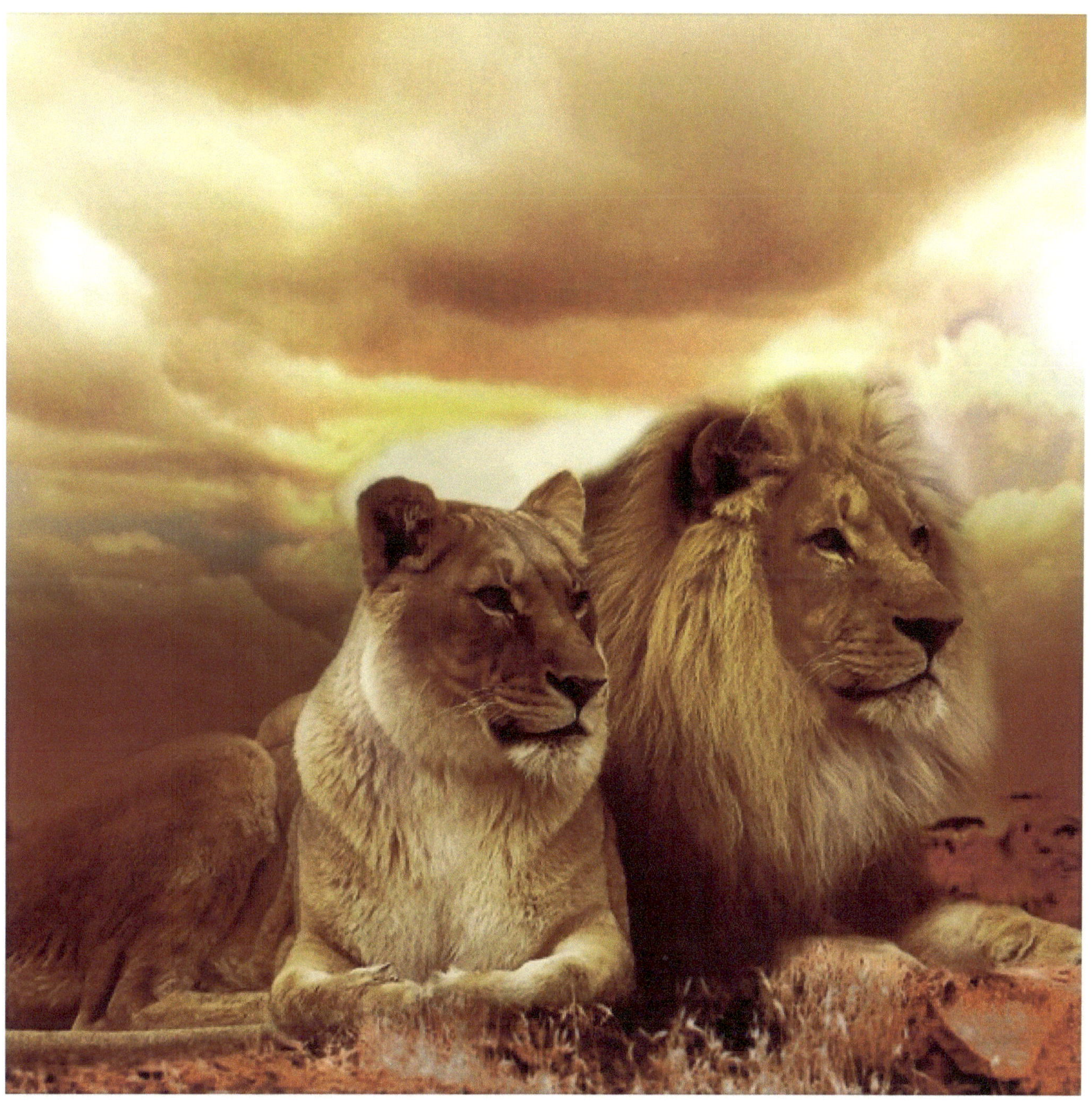

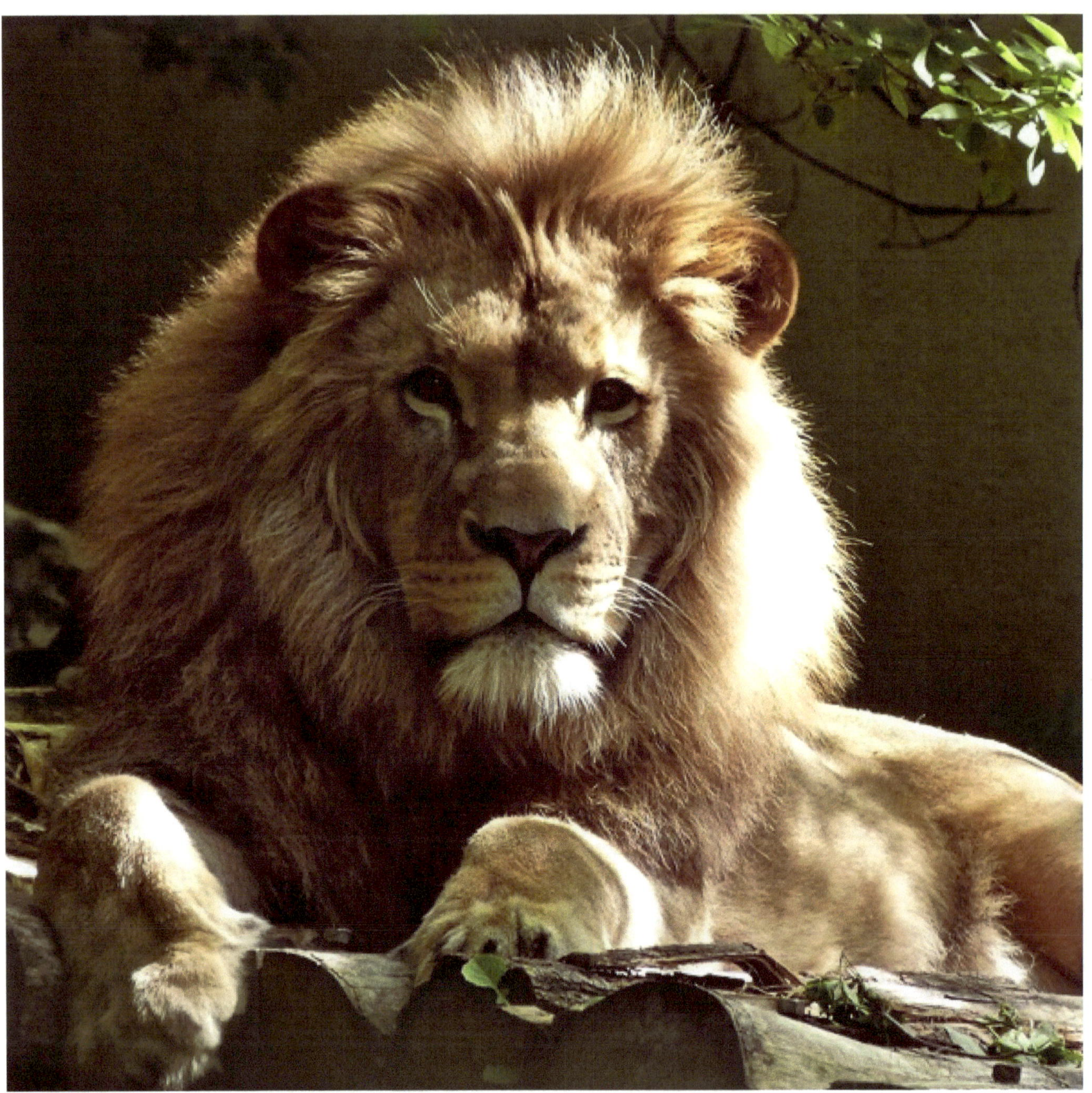

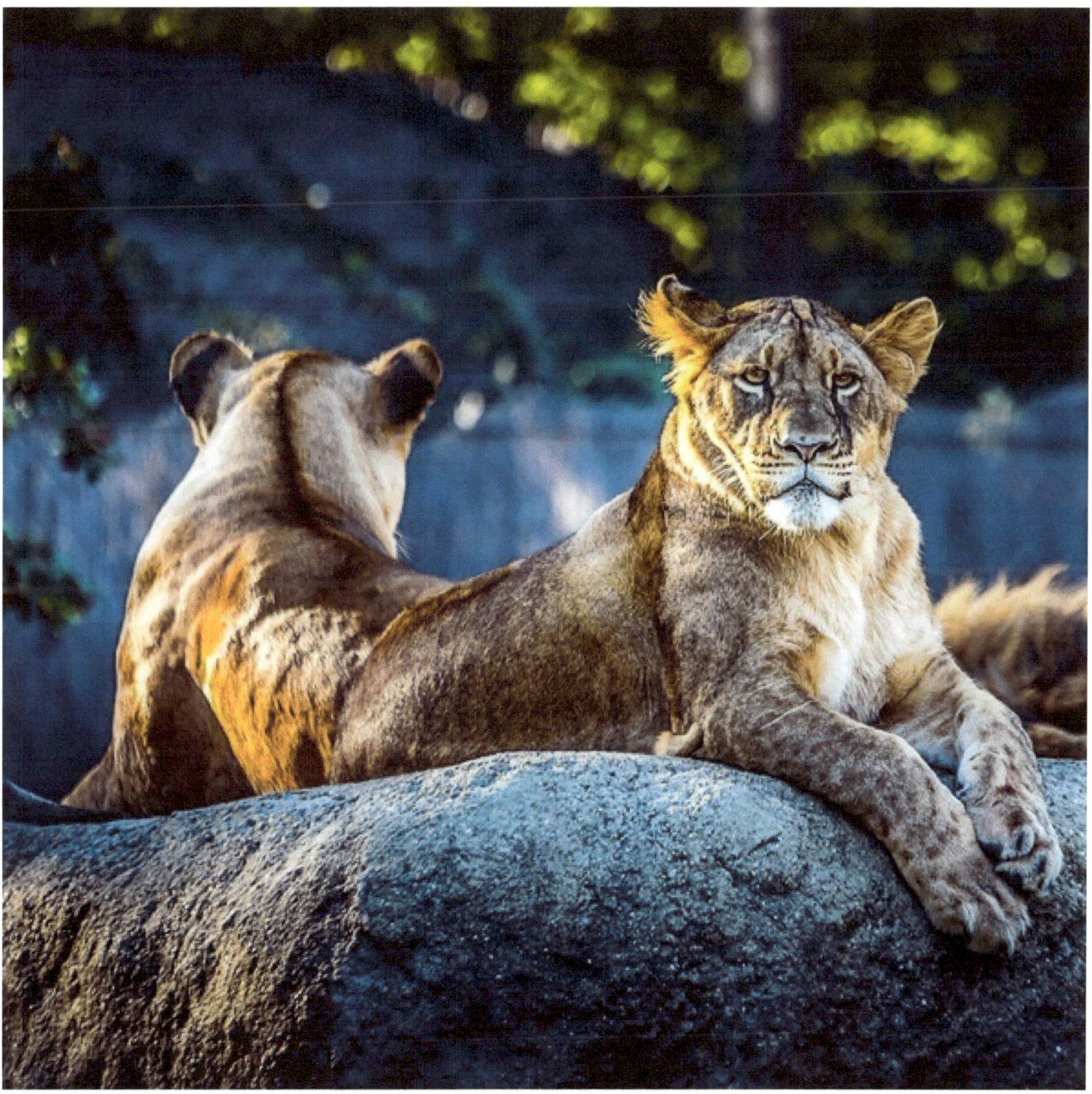

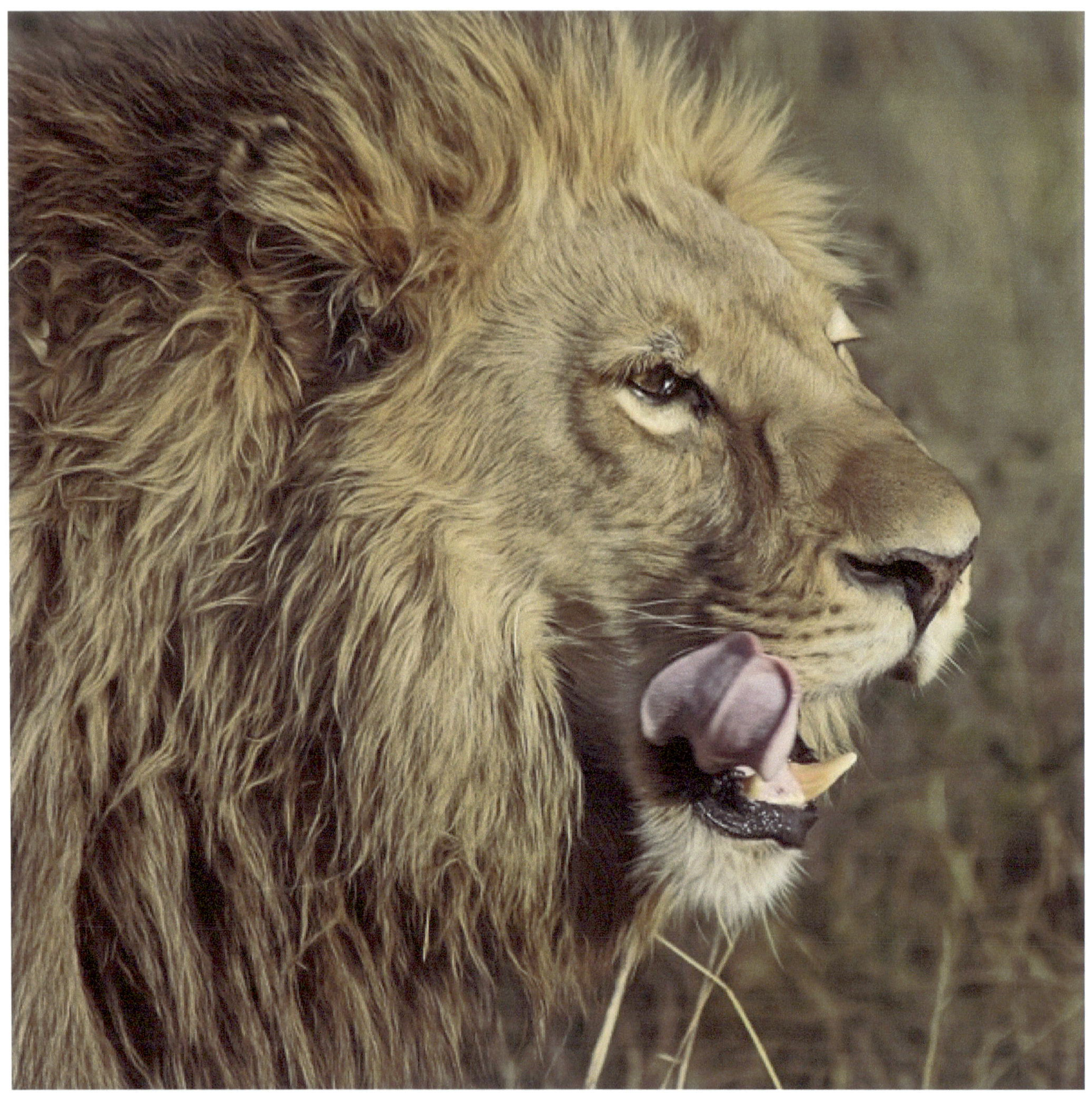

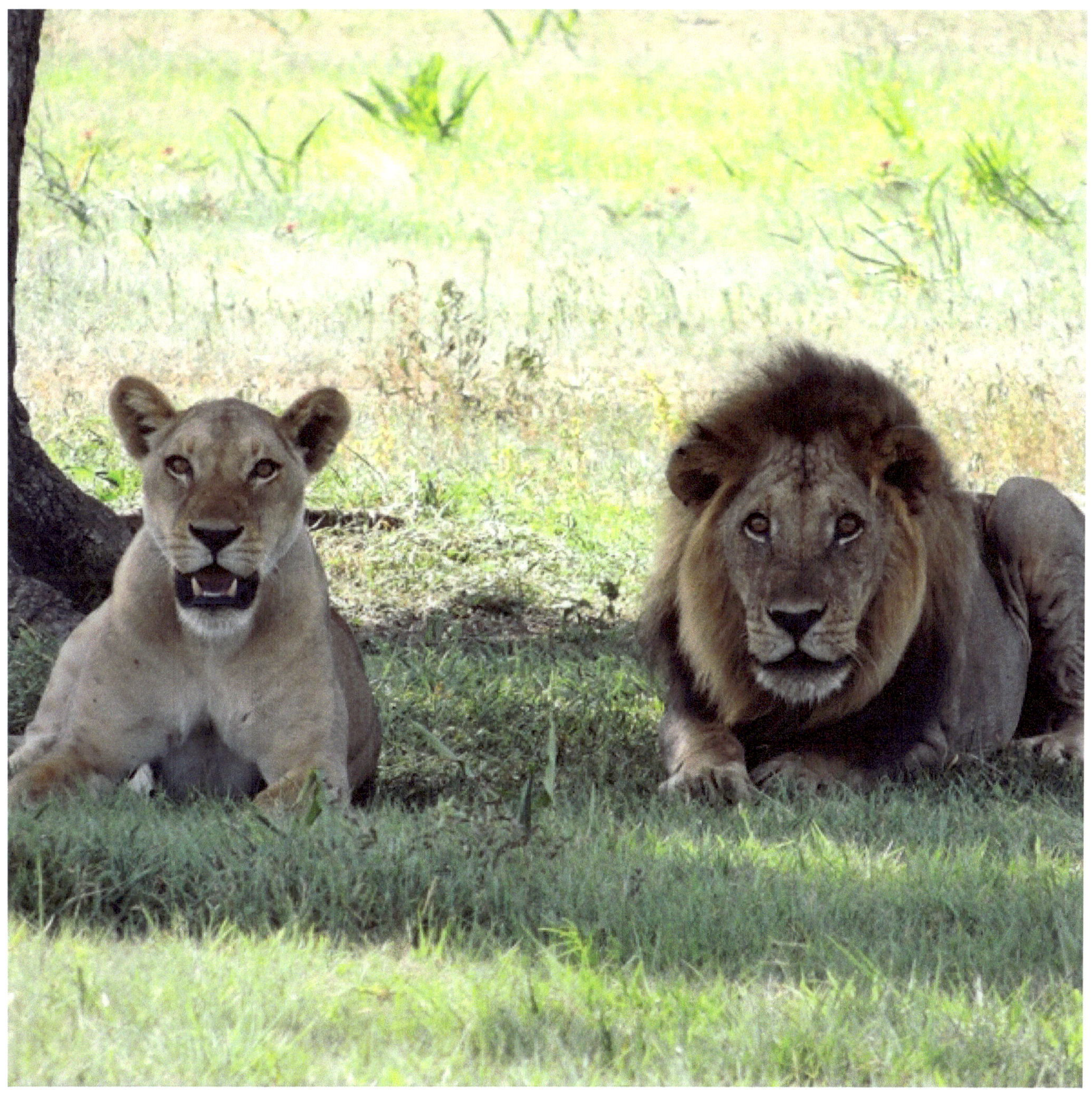

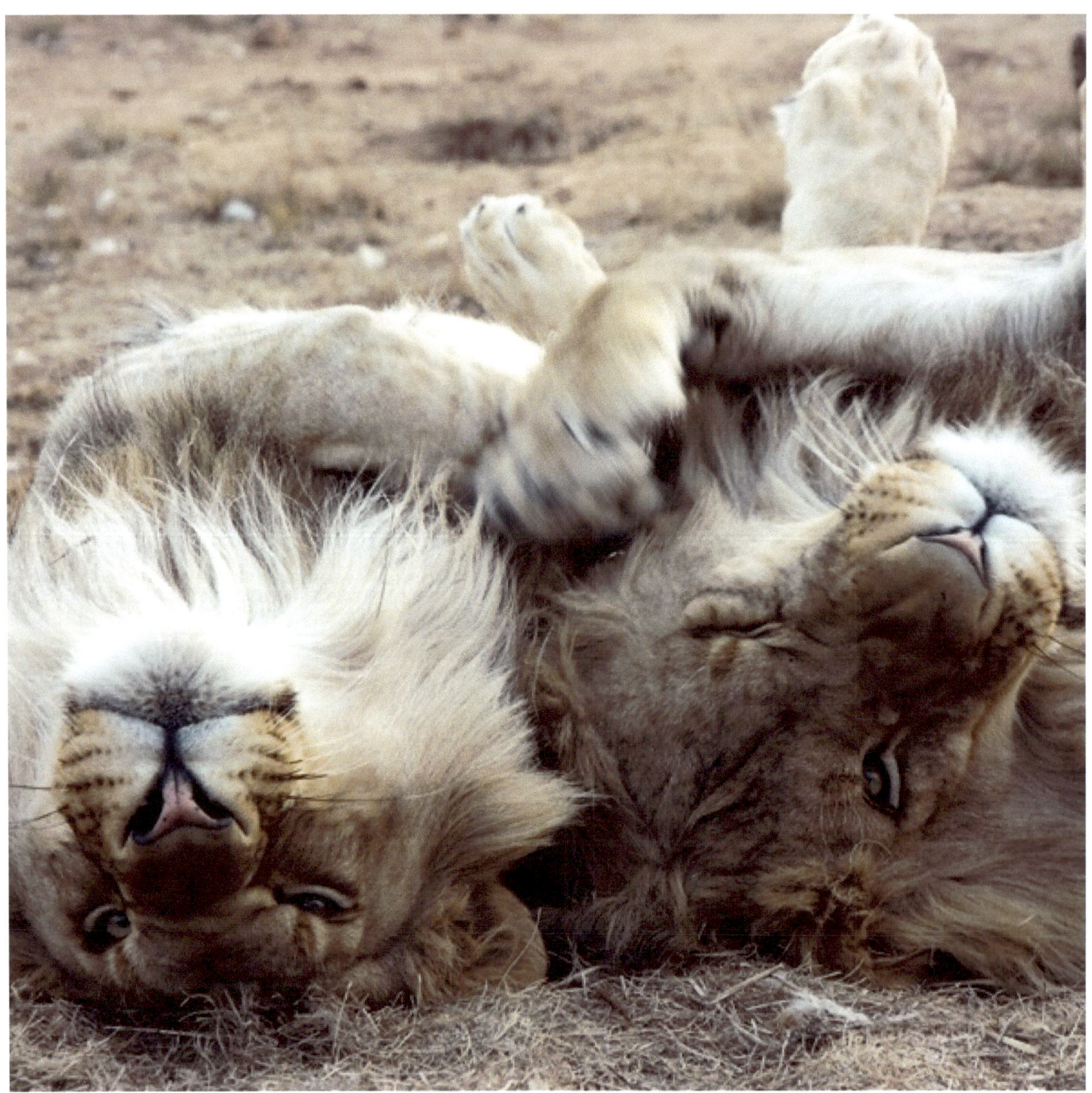

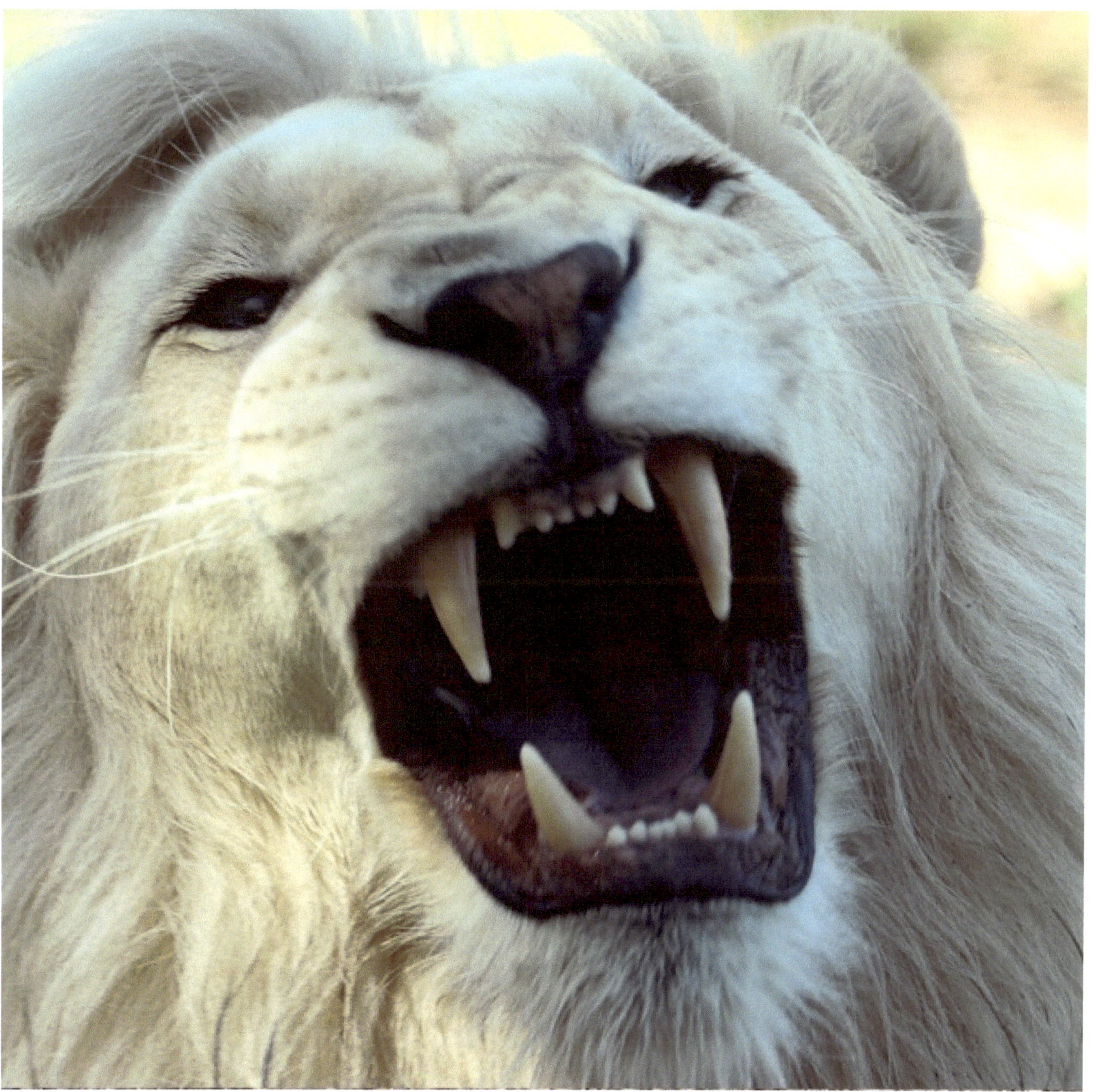

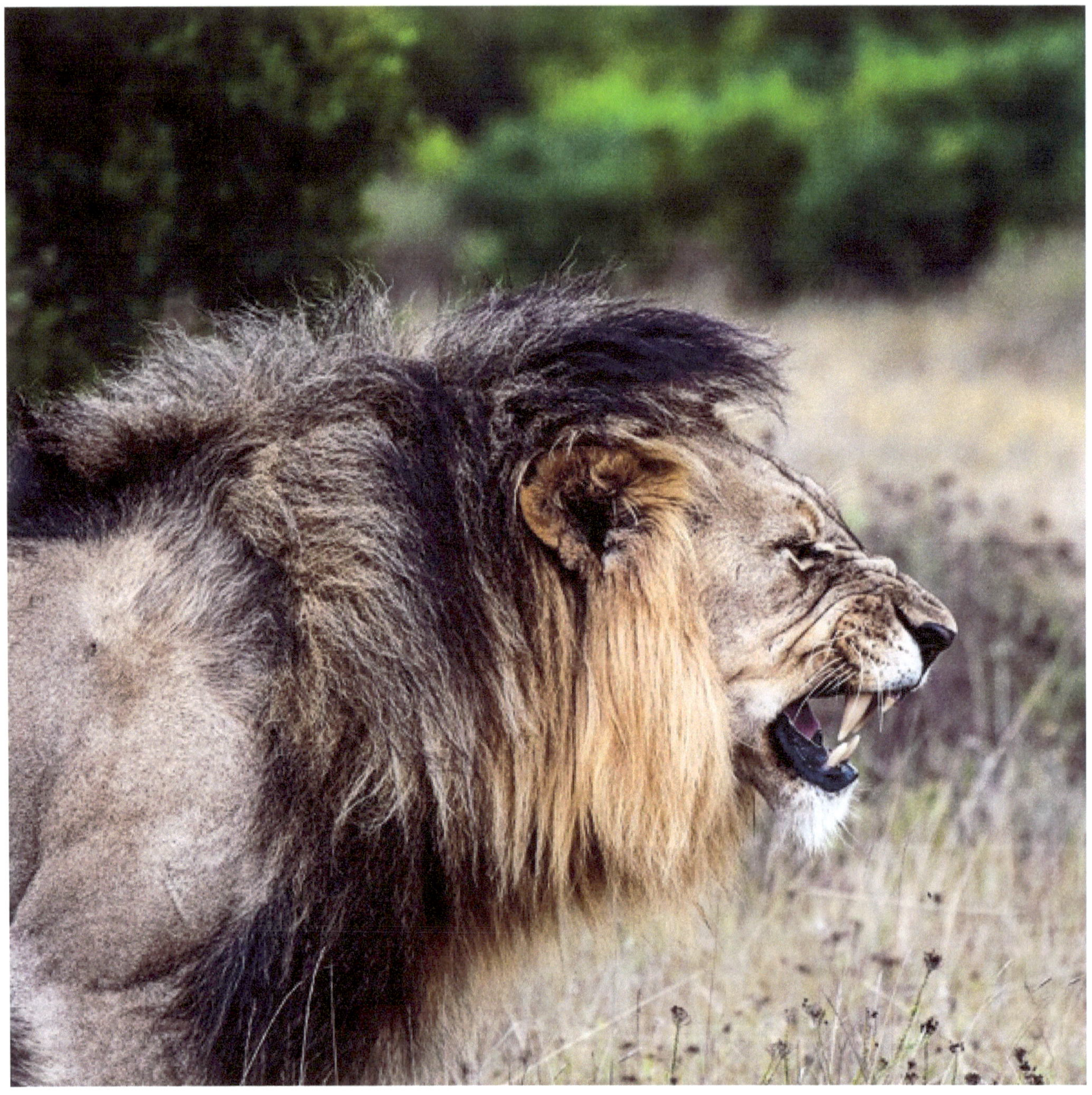

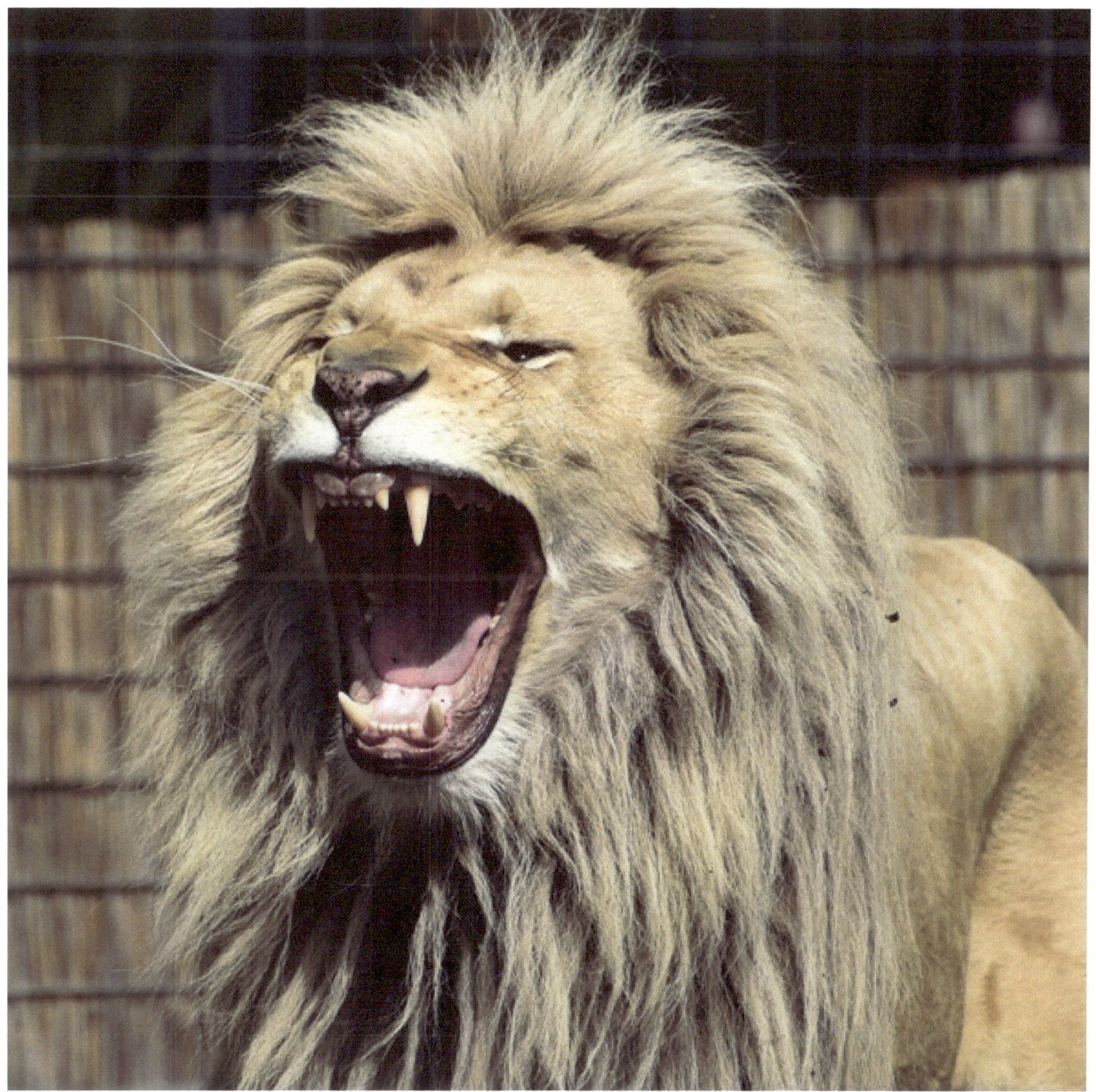

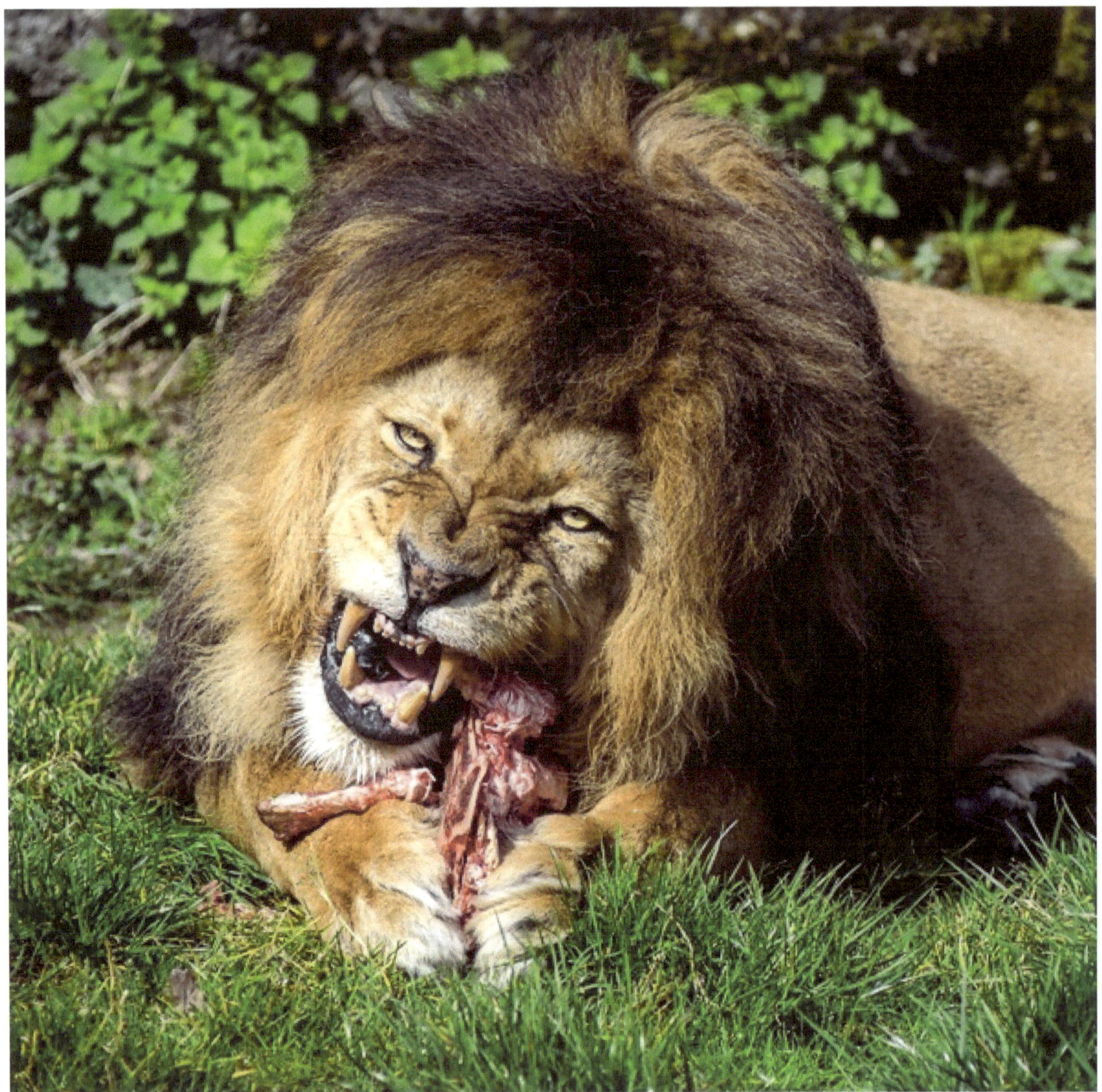

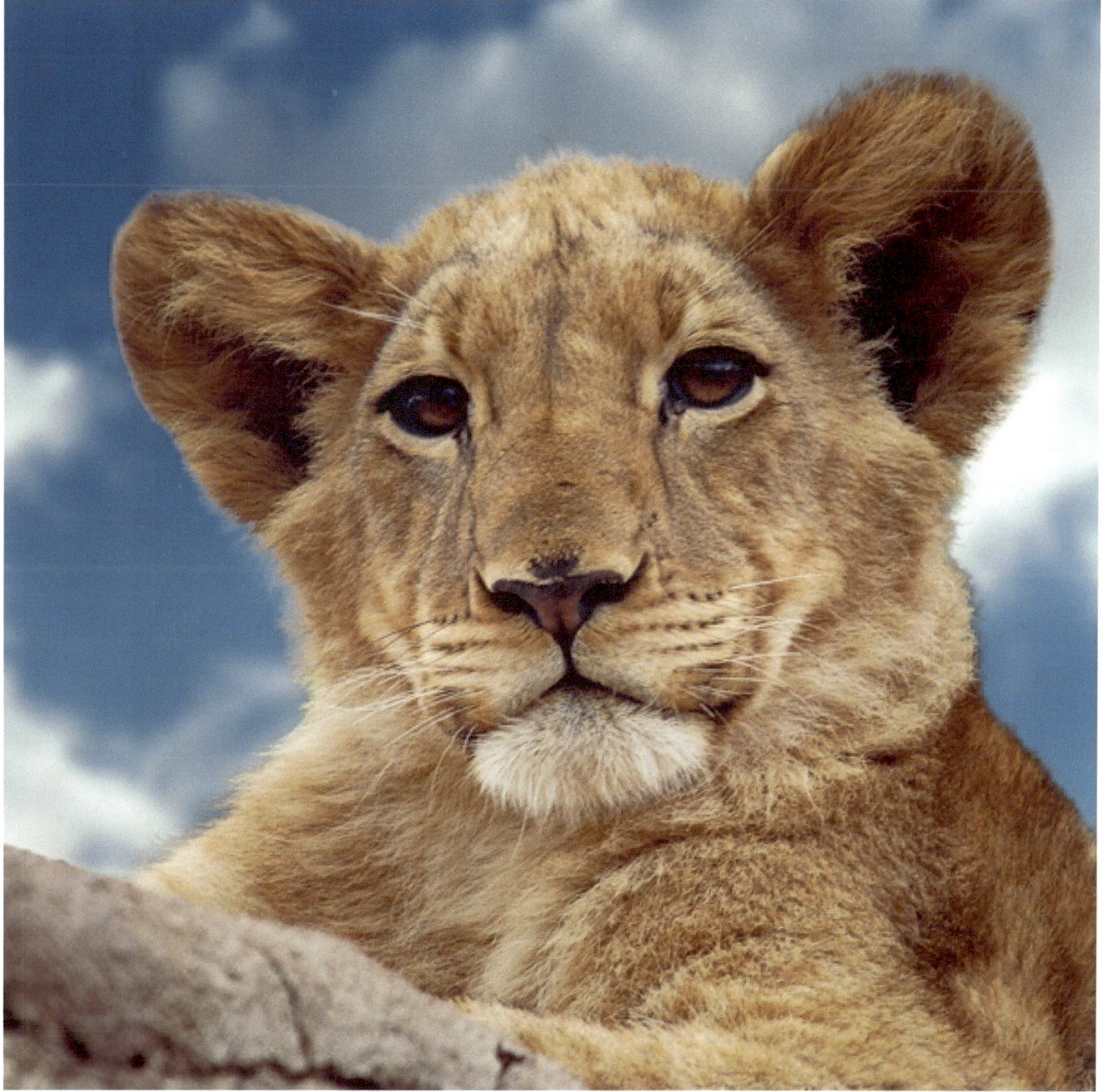

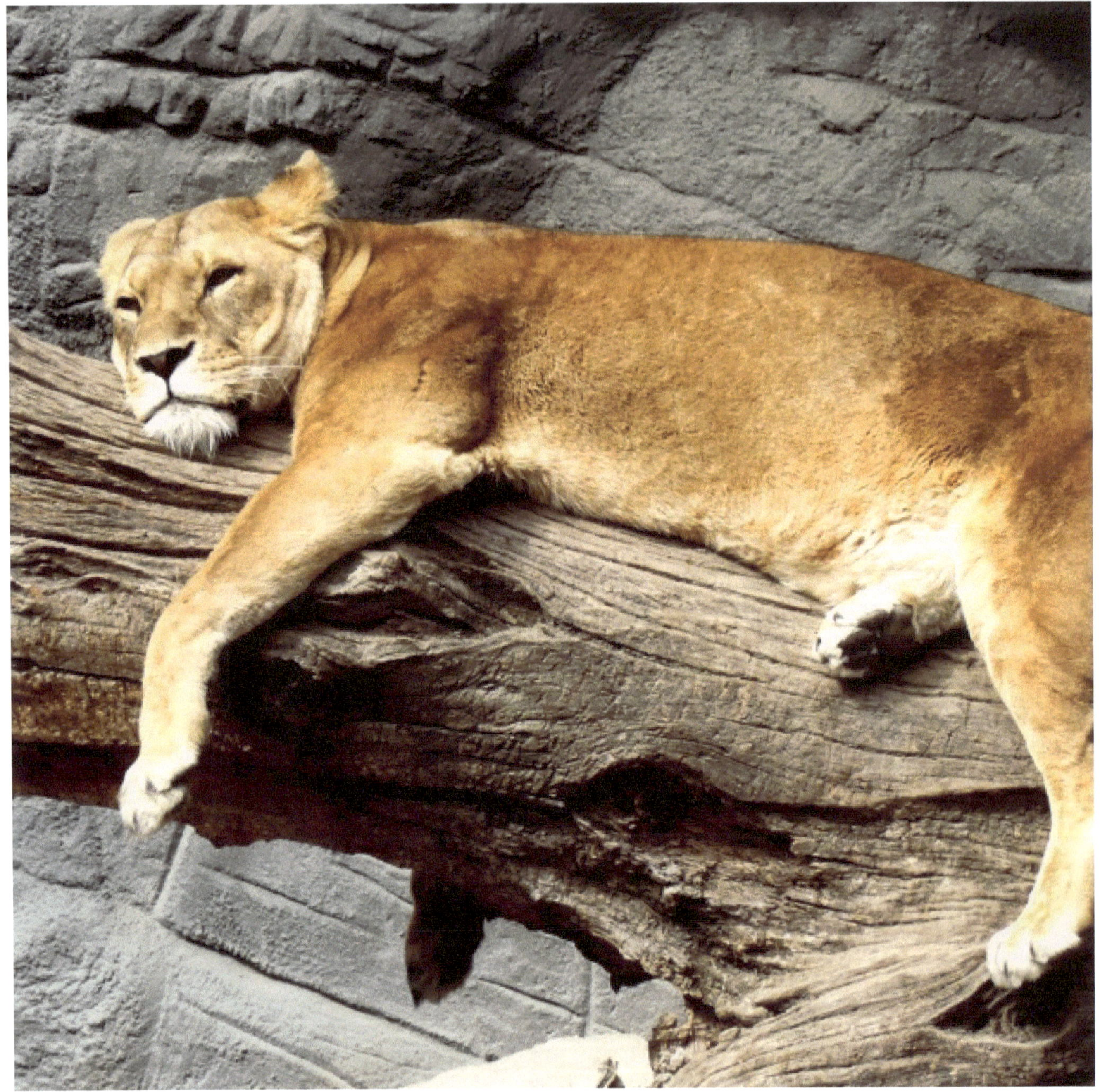

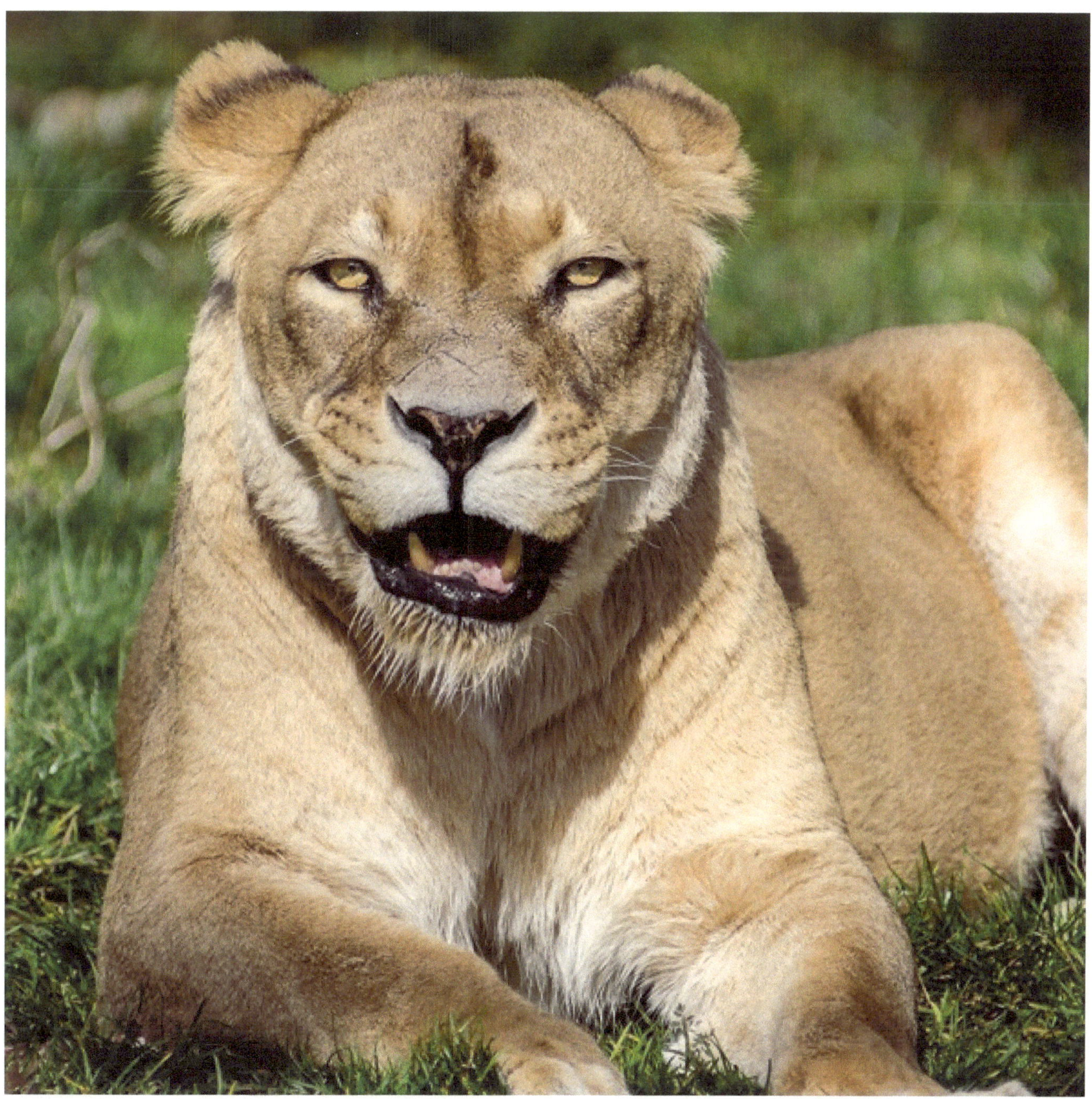

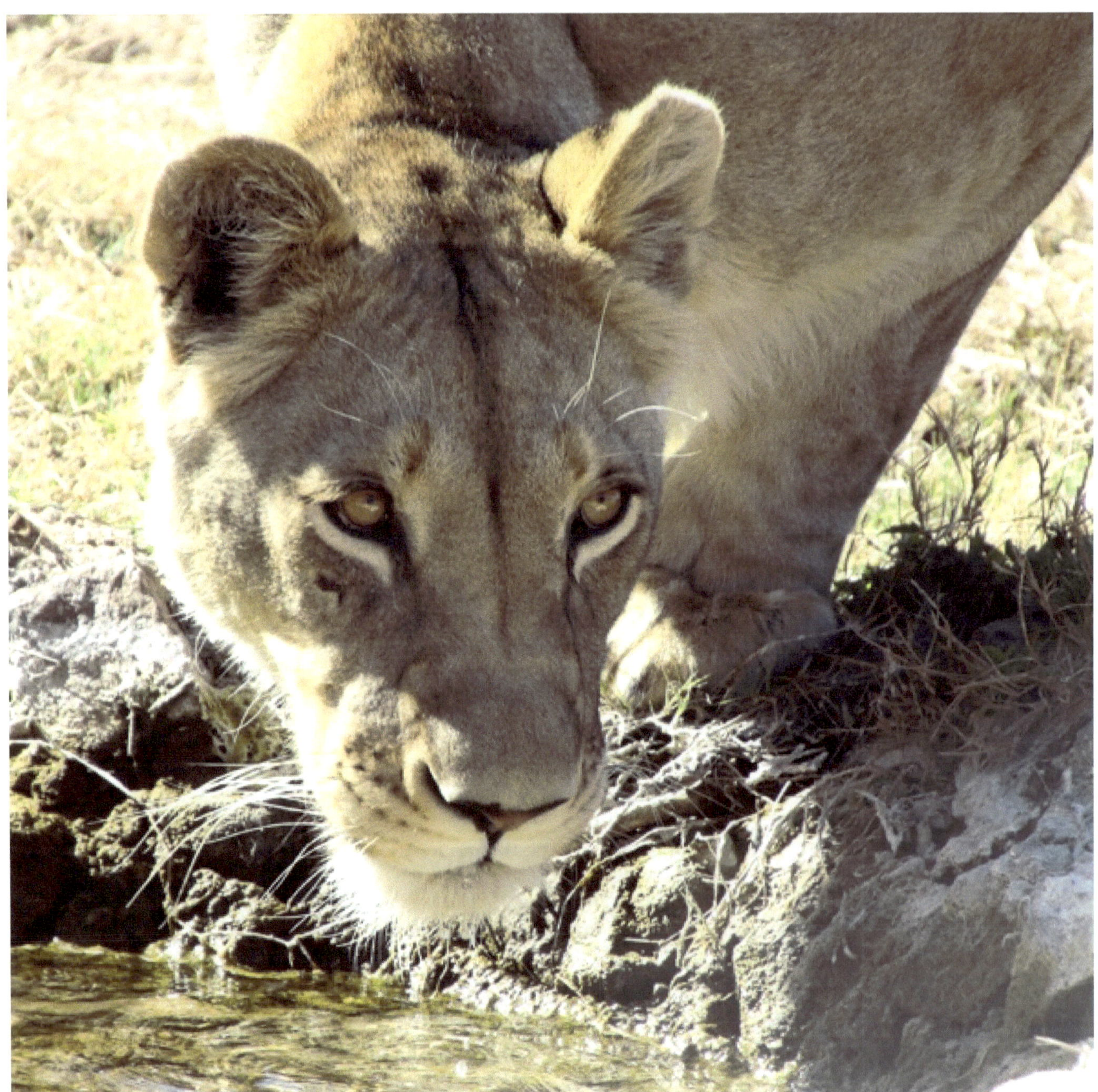

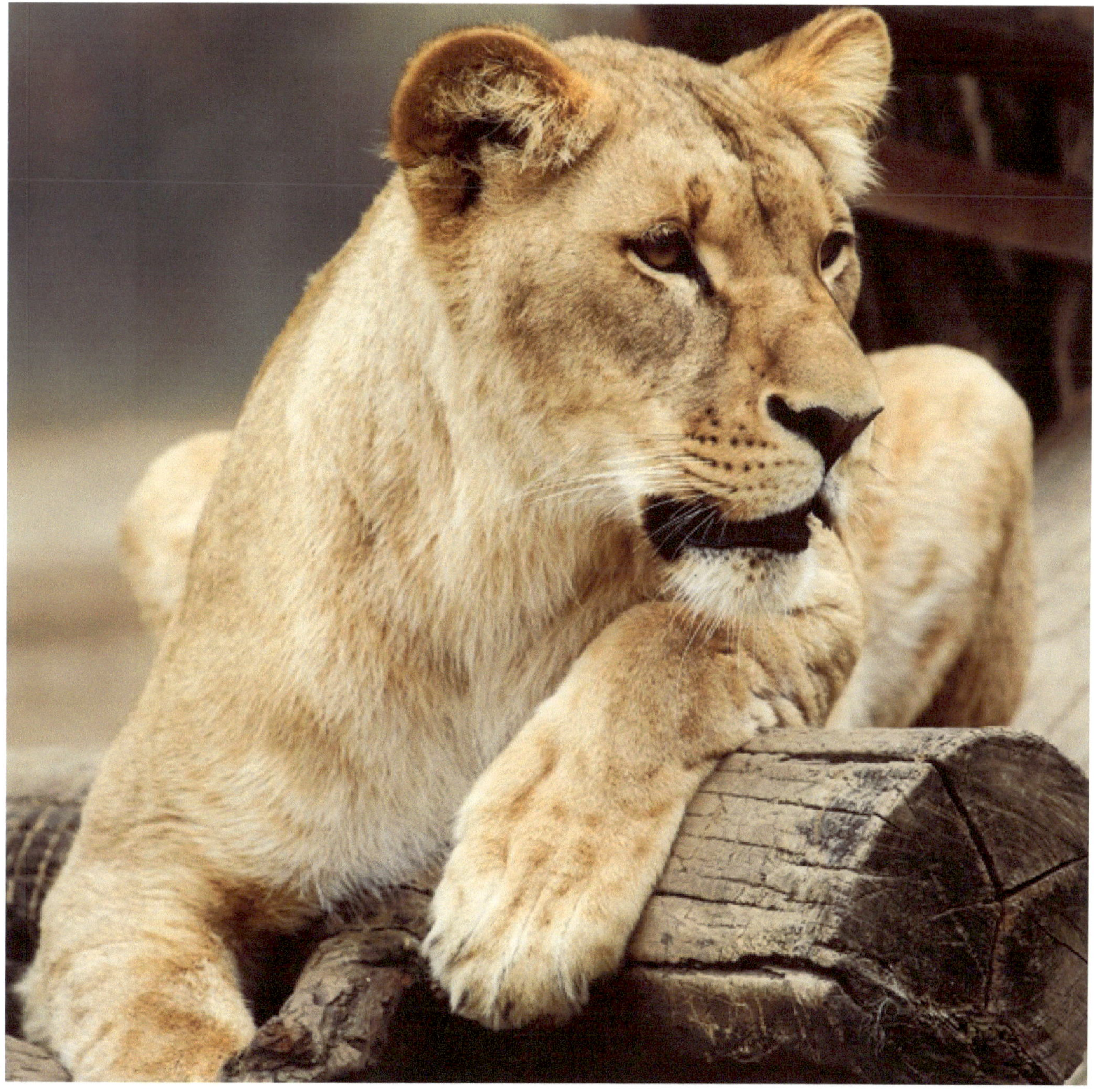

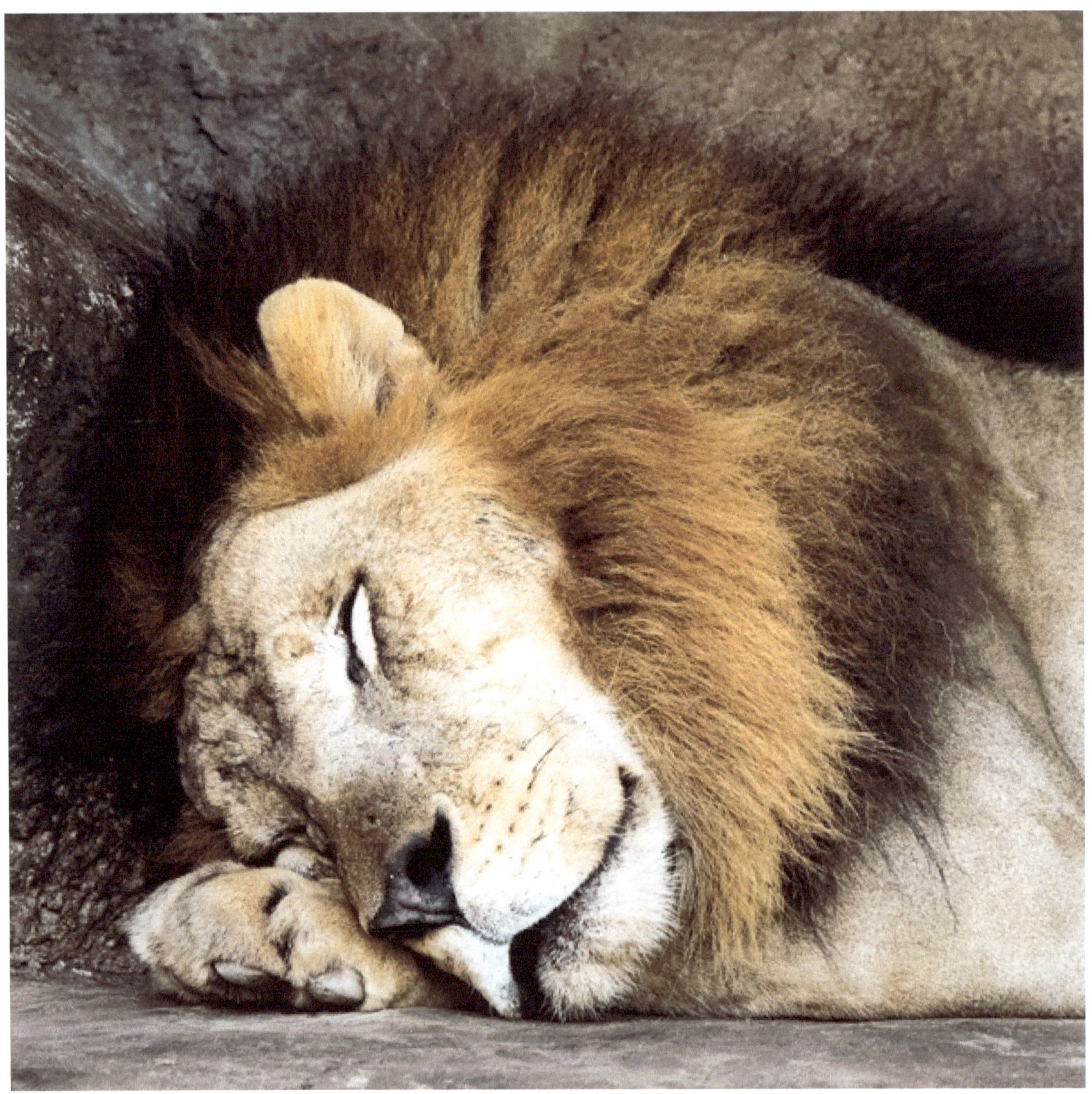

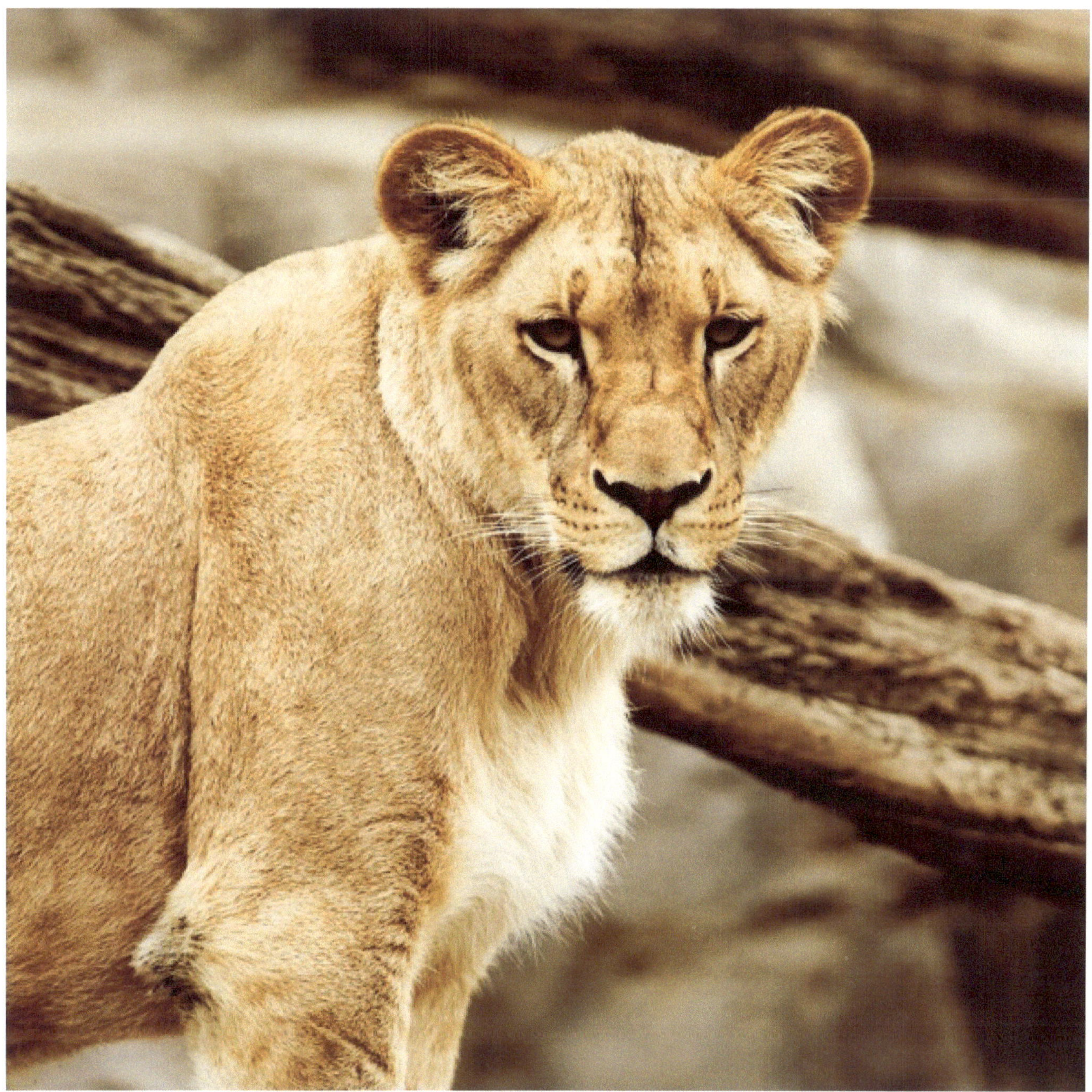

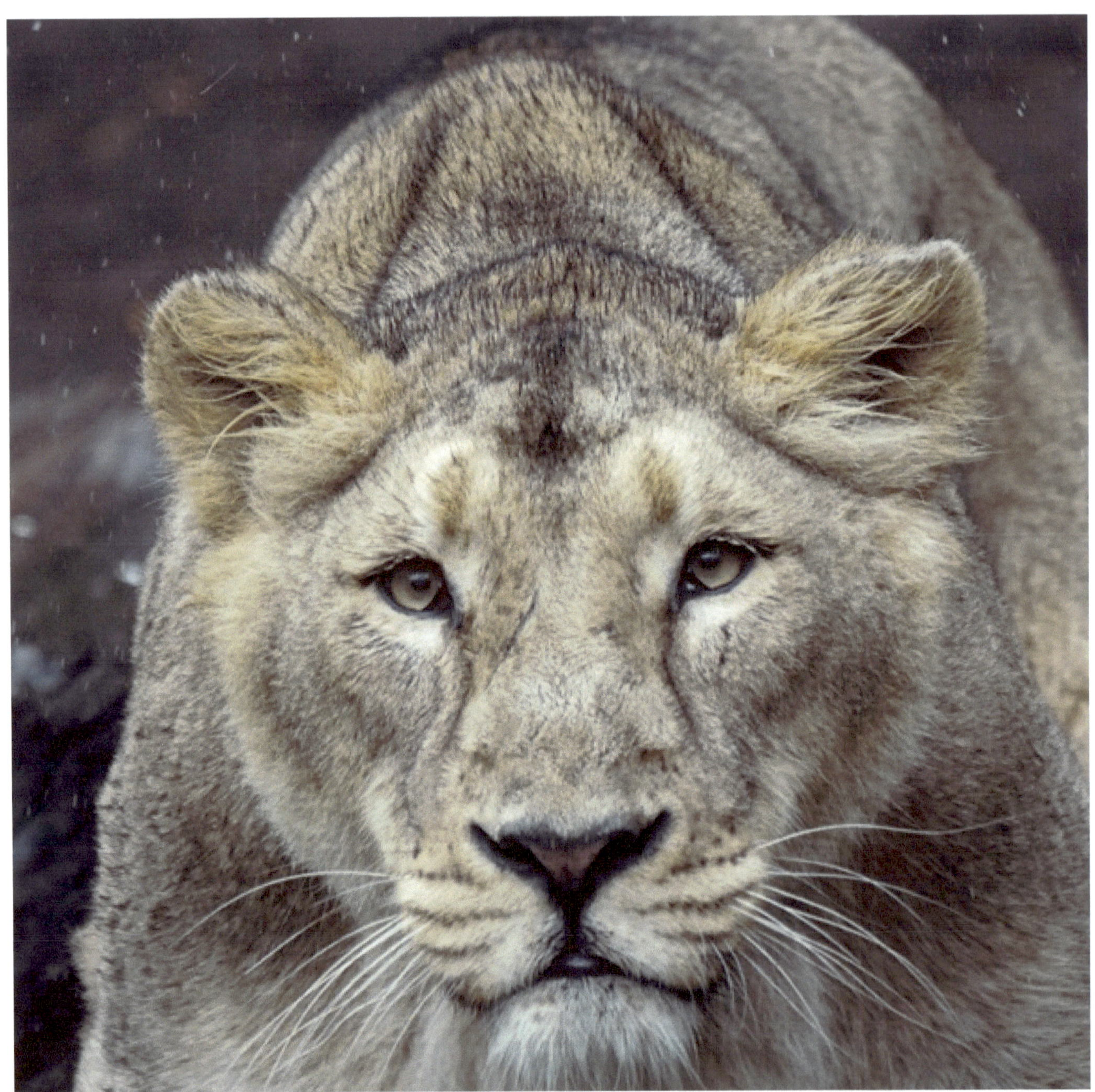

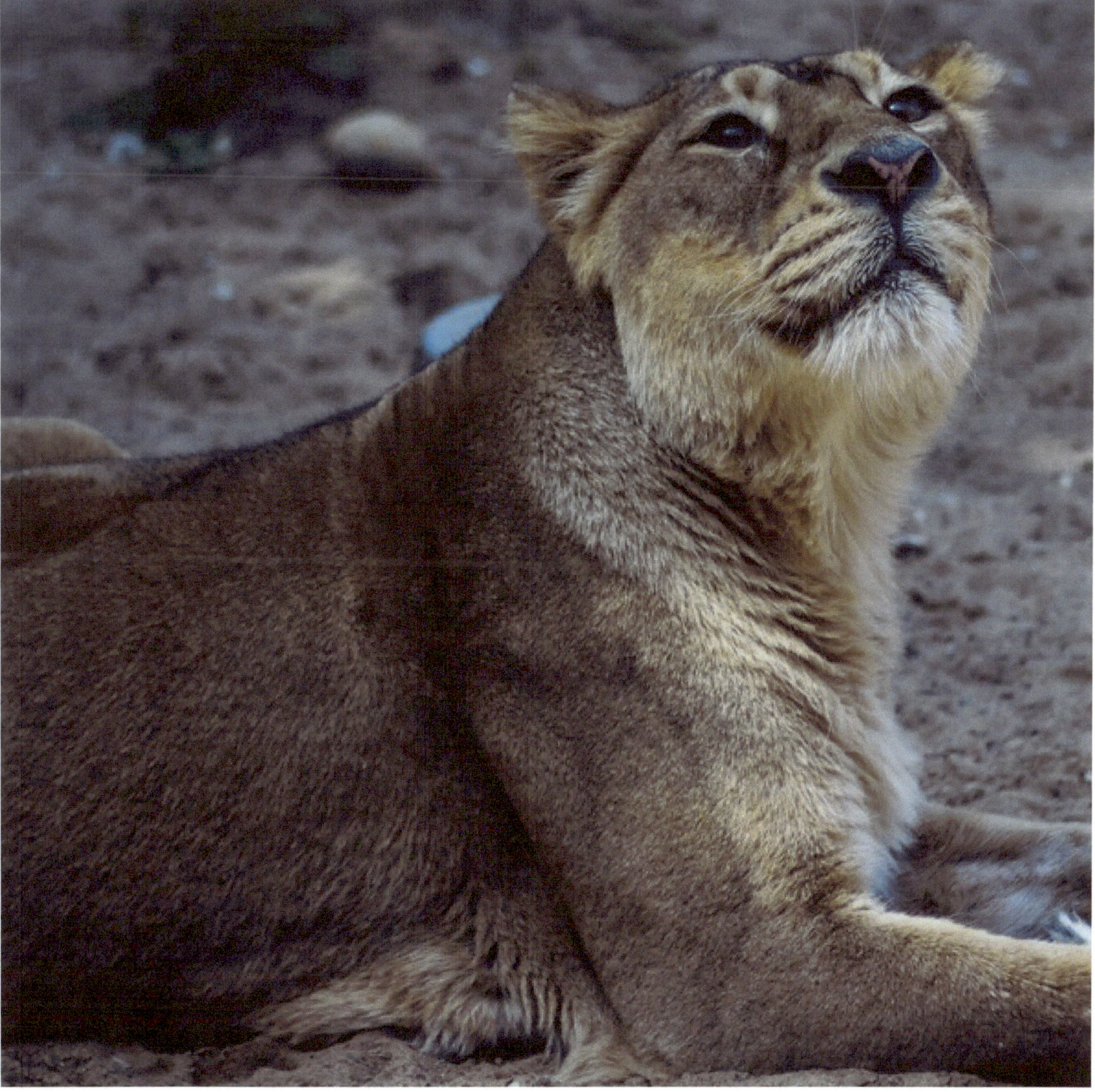

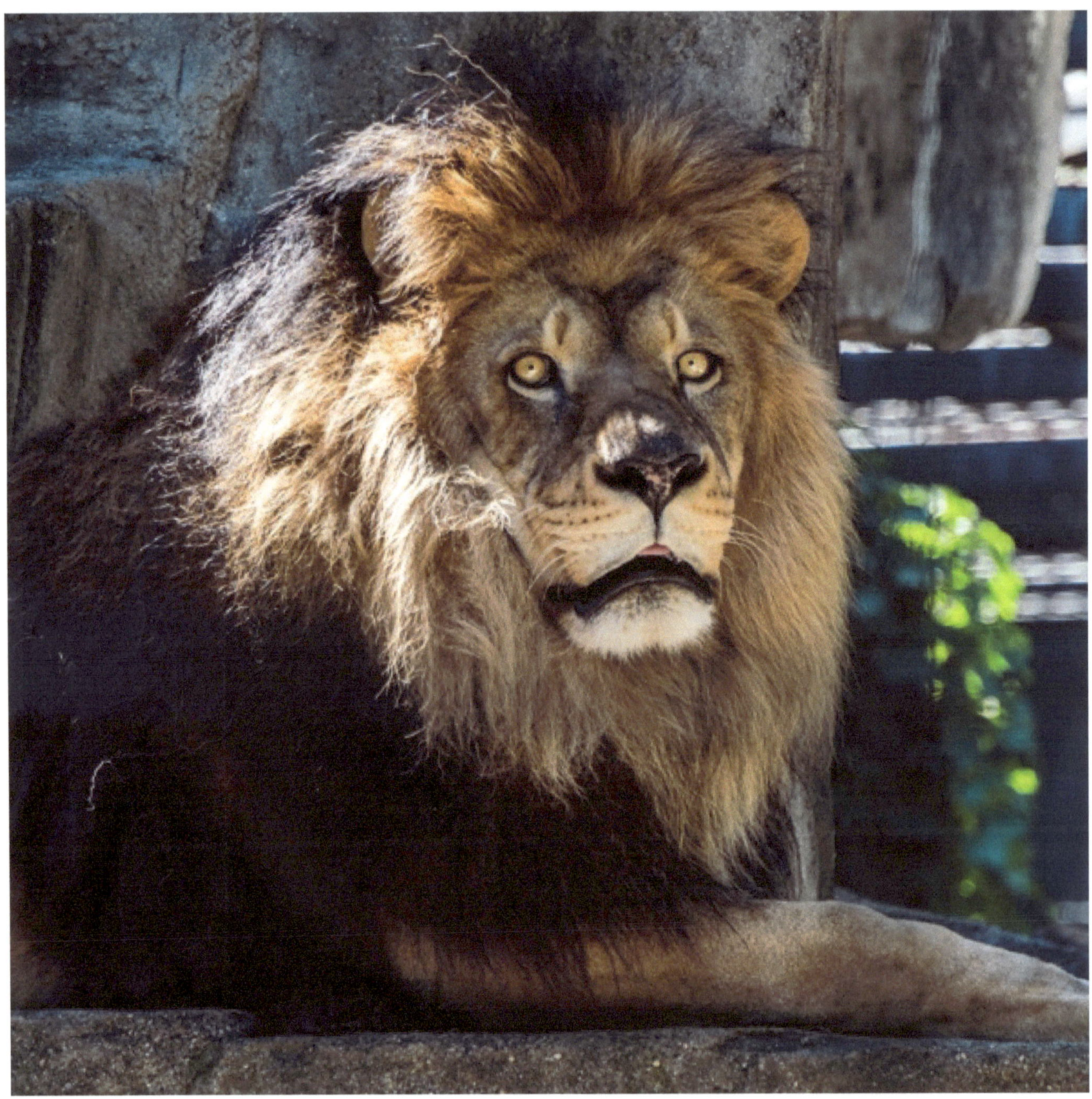

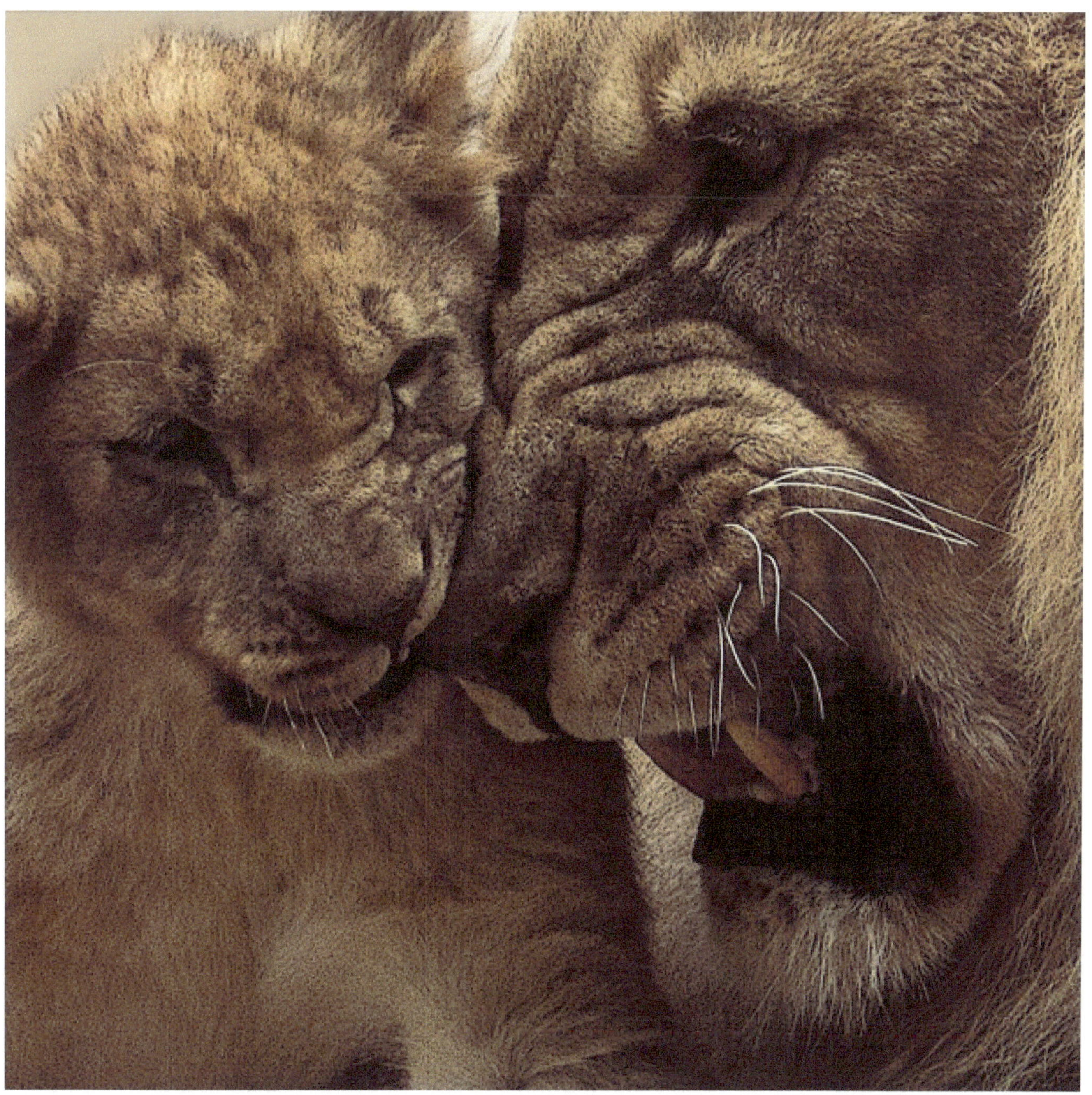

Mick is a lover of Lion's and wanted to create a book of his most favorite pictures to celebrate these beautiful predators.